PRESERVED DIESELS

IN THE UK

Ross Taylor

AMBERLEY

First published 2015

Amberley Publishing
The Hill, Stroud
Gloucestershire, GL5 4EP

www.amberley-books.com

Copyright © Ross Taylor, 2015

The right of Ross Taylor to be identified as
the Author of this work has been asserted in
accordance with the Copyrights, Designs and
Patents Act 1988.

ISBN 978 1 4456 5279 5 (print)
ISBN 978 1 4456 5280 1 (ebook)

British Library Cataloguing in Publication Data.
A catalogue record for this book is available from
the British Library.

Typesetting by Amberley Publishing.
Printed in the UK.

Introduction

This book is intended to give an overview of preserved main line diesel locomotives in Great Britain operating on some of the many heritage railways and, in some cases, the national network. Over the last three decades, a considerable number of locomotives have been saved from the cutters torch after withdrawal from revenue-earning service by British Rail and its private successors. A small number were saved earlier, but in the late 1960s and '70s, when many less successful types were withdrawn, the preservation movement was only interested in the last steam locomotives. Sadly, as a result, several interesting classes were lost.

Of the stock that has survived, many have been restored to their former glory and now work on the many heritage railways up and down the country, many of which hold diesel galas where all trains are diesel-hauled, often with visiting locos from other lines to add interest. A large number of lines also have regular diesel operating days in their normal timetable, usually on the same weekend(s) each month, where members of the public can enjoy haulage and photography of some of the home diesel fleet. 1960s-themed events are also a very popular feature at several lines where both diesel and steam work together, just as they did in steams' last days, often also having displays of period road vehicles at some stations to add interest. The locomotives can also see service at short notice in the event of non-availability of steam traction or in periods of dry weather when the risk of sparks from steam engines poses too great a risk of line side fires.

Some locomotives are also passed for main line operation and see use on charters and tours, and to move convoys of stock to heritage lines for special events. Occasionally, these locomotives have even been hired by main line train operating companies in times of stock shortages, giving much pleasure to enthusiasts who can see them working under somewhat more demanding conditions than the gentle 25 mph maximum legally permitted on a heritage line. Also, in some cases, locos that were preserved have been sold back for main line operation (the English Electric Type 3 Class 37 particularly being favoured), though in many cases there is an agreement that once their second revenue service period ends they will return to preservation. Such sales often raise much needed money to fund further restorations as the vast majority of the engines we enjoy today have been restored by the dedication and fund raising of groups of volunteers, spending hundreds of hours working, often exposed to the elements, to return the locomotives to a high standard both mechanically and cosmetically.

Very few of the people who restore stock or operate heritage railways receive any pay, and we should all be very grateful for their willingness to spend much of their spare time on such duties. Some groups and lines are registered charities but fundraising is an eternal problem for many. Sourcing spare parts for some of the rarer locomotives can also be a major problem – there are cases of parts being obtained from locomotives that are largely similar abroad, and from power units that were originally not in rail use (at least one Napier Deltic 18 engine was acquired from marine use to enable the repair of one in a Class 55). Some locomotives have seen the preservation teams work miracles restoring a derelict wreck that was generally regarded as beyond salvation to a fully working, good-as-new shining machine capable of regular work once again.

In this book, I have attempted to cover a wide variety of locomotive classes and heritage railways, however, due to the aforementioned slow start to diesel preservation, it is inevitable that certain types feature much more heavily than others, as some have but one survivor and not necessarily in operational condition at present. In addition, some heritage lines are much more favourable to diesel operation than others, therefore these lines will tend to be more prominent in the following pictures. Many thanks to Ian Tunstall, Simon Drake and Paul Manley.

Opposite below: Visiting locomotive to the North Yorkshire Moors Railway for the 2015 summer diesel gala is No. 31271. Seen here arriving into Goathland with the 11.59 Pickering to Grosmont service on Saturday 27 June 2015.

Above: Built in 1965 at the Vulcan Foundry, and now based at the North Yorkshire Moors, is fifty-year-old No. 37264. Seen here sitting in Goathland railway station with the 12.33 Grosmont to Pickering service on Saturday 27 June 2015.

Above: Seen sitting in the yard at the Great Central Railway North in Ruddington is No. 37009 (D6709). The locomotive is having some major restoration work done in readiness for the return to service. Seen here on Saturday 27 June 2015.

Above: Part of the East Lancashire Railway diesel group is No. 25054 (D5054), seen here at Barrow Hill Roundhouse near Chesterfield. The locomotive is currently temporarily based here at Barrow Hill while it receives a heavy overhaul. Seen sitting out in the sun on Saturday 18 April 2015. The livery is BR green with yellow warning panels.

Opposite below: Looking a little rough and under the weather is No. 27066, seen here working shuttle services at Barrow Hill Roundhouse rarities gala. Seen here on Saturday 18 April 2015. D832 was on the rear of the train.

Above: EWS-liveried No. 31466 (31115, D5533) is seen approaching Burrs while working the 2J70 15.05 Rawtenstall to Heywood service. The Class 31 is on long-term hire to the East Lancashire Railway from the Dean Forest Railway. Seen here on Friday 3 July 2015. The locomotive was built in Brush Works at Loughborough in 1959.

Below: Purchased from BR in 1992 by SRPS (Scottish Railway Preservation Society) was No. 20020, and it is seen here some twenty-three years later. The locomotive is seen passing Burrs Country Park with the 15.40 2E39 Bury to Ramsbottom shuttle service. Seen here as one of the main star guests to the summer diesel gala and was photographed here on Saturday 4 July 2015.

Above: Scottish Railway Preservation Society No. 26038 is seen arriving into Ramsbottom while in charge of the 2J60 11.15 Rawtenstall to Heywood service. Seen here on Sunday 5 July 2015.

Below: SRPS class No. 47643 is seen arriving into Ramsbottom while in charge of the 11.15 2J60 Rawtenstall to Heywood service. Seen here on Saturday 4 July 2015. The locomotive is based at the Bo'ness & Kinniel Railway but was one of the many visiting locomotives for the 2015 summer diesel gala event.

Above: East Lancashire Railway-based No. 37418 opens up past Burrs while in charge of the 2J71 16.23 Heywood to Rawtenstall service. The train should have been hauled by class mate No. 37025, however problems resulted. Therefore, the ELR beast stepped in. Seen here on Saturday 4 July 2015.

Opposite below: Brush Type 4 No. 47643 powers past Burrs Country Park while in charge of the 2J66 13.33 Rawtenstall to Heywood service. Seen here on Friday 3 July 2015. The Class 47 has come from the Bo'ness & Kinniel Railway and was one of the visiting locomotives along with Nos 26038, 20020, 37025 and 31601.

Above: Hoover No. 50015 *Valiant* is seen departing away from Ramsbottom Goods Loop while working the 2E34 11.48 Ramsbottom to Bury shuttle service. The Class 50 is based here at the East Lancashire Railway and is seen on Saturday 4 July 2015.

Above: The East Lancashire Railway held its summer diesel gala over the weekend of 4-6 July. Here we can see visiting locomotive No. 37324 arriving into Irwell Vale with the 10.15 Rawtenstall to Heywood service. Photographed here on the second day, 5 July 2014.

Above: BR Blue-liveried Sulzer No. 45108 sits at Swanwick Junction on the Midland Railway Centre in Butterly, awaiting to depart the depot to work the day's diesel-hauled services. Seen here on Saturday 18 April 2015.

Opposite below: No. 50017 is seen heading away from Preston while working the 17.03 0Z50 Washwood Heath Met Cammel to Bo'ness Jn Exchange sidings. Seen here on Thursday 23 July 2015. The train was taking Nos 50007, 40106 and 50017 to the Bo'ness & Kinniel Railway ready for the summer diesel gala.

Above: Based at the East Lancs is No. 37109, seen here dragging a poorly No. 37025 as it arrives into Ramsbottom. The train was the 2J62 12.01 Rawtenstall to Heywood service. Seen here on Saturday 4 July 2015.

Above: After being built in 1963 at Derby was BR Blue No. 25059. Seen here on the Keighley & Worth Valley Railway as it approaches into Keighley with a service from Oxenhope. Seen here on 27 May 2012.

Opposite below: Nos 73001 and 20020 power past Burrs while working the 2J68 14.19 Rawtenstall to Heywood service. Seen here over the East Lancashire Railway diesel gala weekend. Photographed on 4 July 2015.

Above: Scottish-based No. 26038 *Tom Clift* powers past Burrs while working the slightly delayed 13.33 2J66 Rawtenstall to Heywood service. Seen here on Saturday 4 July 2015.

Below: BR Blue No. 25059 (D5209) is seen thrashing out of Keighley while in charge of the first train to Oxenhope. Seen here on 27 May 2012. The Type 2 locomotive was built by BR in Derby in 1963 and from there the locomotive was sent to the nearby Toton depot. The loco worked its first service across the line on the 10 October 1987 when it was being trailed.

Above: The newest locomotive to the diesel fleet at the Keighley & Worth Valley Railway is No. 37075, which is seen here at Keighley as it runs around its train. The locomotive was built in 1962 by English Electric and was allocated to Teesside's Thornaby depot. The locomotive was purchased in 1999 from EWS for preservation and travelled to many preserved railways before being based at Keighley. Photographed here on 27 May 2012.

Below: No. 20031 (D8031) is photographed here departing Keighley with a service to Oxenhope. The locomotive, which has been based at the railway since August 1992, is still in regular use and is photographed here on 25 May 2012.

Above: British Rail Class 14 are small diesel hydraulic locomotives that were produced in 1960. Only twenty-six of the locomotives were ordered at first. However, the order was expanded from twenty-six to fifty-six in 1963, before the first batch had started being built at British Railways Swindon Works. There are currently only nineteen of the locos saved from scrap and only twelve in fully working order. No. 14901 (D9524) is seen sitting at Rowsley depot at Peak Rail near Matlock, Derbyshire. Seen here on 18 April 2015.

Opposite below: After being purchased from Toton in 1991, No. 20110 (D8110) was based at the South Devon Railway for many years. The locomotives is seen here passing Riverford Bridge near Staverton. Seen here on 10 July 2005.

Above: Coal Sector No. 20031 is seen running around its train at Keighley with star guest No. 57007 from DRS (Direct Rail Services). The double-header was starring in the diesel gala, seen here on 7 June 2009.

Above: Choppers Nos 20118 and 20227 power away from Buckfastleigh on the South Devon Railway with a service to Totnes. Seen here on 10 July 2005.

Below: Great Central Railway North's choppers D8154 and D8007 arrive into Swanwick Junction on the Midland Railway Centre with a service to Butterly. The locomotives were guests for the 'Chopperfest', among a few other Class 20 diesel locomotives. Seen here on 20 May 2007.

Above: Choppers Nos 20227 and 20118 arrive into Buckfastleigh on the South Devon Railway with a service from Totnes. Seen here on 10 July 2005. The locomotives are both main line registered and have been noted on the tube stock moves for GBRF and RHTT duties in the past for DB Schenker.

Below: Sulzer No. 33103 powers up the steep gradient away from Keighley on the Keighley & Worth Valleys diesel gala. The train was the 10.20 to Oxenhope. The locomotive was built in 1960 by the Birmingham Railway Carriage & Wagon Company (BRCW) in Smethwick and at the time carried the number D6514.

Above: English Electric No. 37418 powers away from Irwell Vale with the 2J60 11.15 Rawtenstall to Heywood service. The locomotive is currently based at the East Lancashire Railway and in 2010 received a major overhaul due to a serious power unit failure. The locomotive returned to traffic five years later in 2015 when it made an appearance on the spring diesel gala on 7 and 8 March. It returned to traffic in its new BR Large Logo livery without names, numbers or logos. Seen here on 30 September 2009.

Opposite below: Napier Deltic thrash reverberates around the valley as D9016 powers past Ewood Bridge near Irwell Vale as it strides for Rawtenstall with the first service of Saturday morning during the ELR summer diesel gala. Seen here on 2 July 2011.

Above: Main line registered Deltic D9000/55022 *Royal Scots Grey* puts its Napier power to the rail as it accelerates away from the 20 mph slack at Eldroth while working 5Z31 10.36 Carnforth to Doncaster West Yard ECS movement. The train will form Spitfire Railtour's 'The Devonian' from Doncaster to Paignton the following morning on Saturday 9 July 2011.

Above: No. 37321 *Loch Treig* (37037 or D6737) looks in a super condition as it passes under Riverford Bridge near Staverton while taking part in the South Devon Railway's diesel gala. Seen here on 10 July 2005.

Above: No. 50042 *TRIUMPH* trundles towards Bodmin General with a very lightweight service from Bodmin Parkway. The locomotive was purchased in 1991 by the Bodmin and Wenford diesel group from Laira depot in Plymouth and arrived at Bodmin in March 1992.

Opposite below: No. 37314, otherwise known as No. 37190 *Dalzell*, coasts away from Buckfastleigh on the South Devon Railway's diesel gala, seen here passing Nursery Pool on 10 July 2005.

Above: No. 33109, also known as a 'Bagpipe' – this is because of the high level brake pipe/ jumper cable fitted to the front of the locomotive. Here we see the Crompton thrashing past Townsend Fold with the 16.30 Rawtenstall–Bury service. Seen here on 15 August 2010.

Above: Visiting from the South Devon Railway was Derby Works-built D7612, paired up with resident No. 25059 while working an Oxenhope to Keighley service during the 2008 diesel gala. D7612, also known as No. 25262, has strong links with Carlisle Kingmoor depot, being renumbered in December 1985 as No. 25901, and was dedicated to mineral and chemical sector traffic. In 1987 the plug was pulled on all Class 25s left in traffic, meaning No. 25901 was stored at Carlisle until 1989, when it was transferred south to Crewe for scrapping at Vic Berry's. Luckily, HNRC (Harry Needle) stepped in to save it and bring the nicknamed 'RAT' back to life. Seen here on 6 June 2008.

Opposite below: Due to a shortage of steam power on the East Lancashire Railway No. 20087 was brought in to cover the steam workings and is seen here in charge of the slightly late running 15.40 Rawtenstall–Heywood service. The loco arrived at the East Lancashire Railway in 1999 where it is based. Seen here on 15 August 2010.

Above: Owned by the National Railway Museum is D1023 *Western Fusilier*, seen here putting its twin Maybach engines to good use as it shatters the peace leaving Haworth for Oxenhope. The locomotive was a star guest to the Keighley & Worth Valley's diesel gala and is seen here on 6 June 2008.

Below: During the 2005 diesel gala on the Gloucester & Warwickshire Railway, No. 24081 (D5081) powers past Hailes while working a Toddington to Cheltenham Racecourse passenger service. The Class 24 is privately owned and is a permanent resident at the GWR. The loco was preserved in 1981 and has remained operational throughout its preservation life.

Above: Looking mighty fine in two-tone green with working headcode panel is Brush Type 4 No. 47004 as it is seen heading into Holywell Halt with a service from Bolton Abbey to Embsay. The Class 47 had been purchased from EWS and is now owned by Newton Heath Diesel Traction Group.

Below: While in charge of the first train of the day, it also has the job of clearing all the snow off the lines. Here we see No. 47402 (D1501), former *Gateshead*, as it powers past Ewood Bridge on its way to Rawtenstall. Seen here on 9 January 2010.

Above: Power to the rails as No. 56003's turbos kick in with the unforgettable scream and the engine's big ends start to throb, making for a spirited and audible departure from a signal check at Townsend Fold after just departing from Rawtenstall with a service to Bury. The locomotive is no longer preserved after being sold for commercial use in 2008. The grid is now owned by DCR and is run under the number 56312.

Above: No. 345 (40145) heads the 1Z28 Carnforth to Castleton Hopwood GF one-way railtour through Giggleswick. The Class 40 is based at the East Lancashire Railway and is main line registered. Seen here on 6 June 2014. West Coast Railways' No. 57315 was on the rear.

Opposite below: Former ScotRail push-pull fitted No. 47715 *Haymarket* leads the newly painted EWS executive Mk2s past Newton-Le-Willows in Richmonshire, North Yorkshire while taking part in the Wensleydale Railway diesel gala. Seen here on 20 September 2008.

Above: Ex-Royal Train locomotive No. 47798 *Prince William* waits on platform 10 at York station. The train was the 5Z69 13.36 empty stock move to Holgate sidings from York. The Class 47 is based at the National Railway Museum. Photographed here on 12 March 2015.

Below: Owned by the Stratford 47 Group is Class 47 No. 47580, seen here stepping in for a steam locomotive while working West Coast Railways' The Waverley, which runs from Carlisle to York. The train is seen here with the return working the 1Z71 and is pictured at Settle Junction. Seen here on 20 July 2014.

Above: Great Central Railway North at Ruddington is the home of Brush Type 4 No. 47292, seen here sitting in the yard supporting its Large Logo livery. Also, No. 20154 sits looking like it needs a lick of paint awaiting its next duty. The Class 20 is owned by the English Electric Preservation Group.

Below: Barrow Hill Roundhouse near Chesterfield, Derbyshire has a variety of many diesel classes. Here we can see the yard full of both commercial and preserved locomotives including electrics. Here we can see preserved Nos 37275, 45060, 55019, D1015 and 56006 all starring in the Type 5 diesel gala. Other locomotives included Nos 66433, 66841, 47818 and many more. Seen here on 8 August 2009.

Above: After being built at the Vulcan Foundry in August 1963, No. 37674 was delivered to British Rail and first allocated to Landore depot at Swansea. Through the loco's life it had been renumbered twice before becoming No. 37674 – former numbers were D6889 and 37169. After being withdrawn from service in December 2004, the locomotive was finally purchased and saved from scrap by Graham Harris in May 2007. The locomotive was moved to Kirkby Stephen East, a small railway where the loco was stored. In 2014, the locomotive was removed and sent to the Wensleydale Railway for restoration work. Photographed here on 4 June 2007.

Opposite below: Sitting in the early morning sun is restored No. 37294, the locomotive sports BR Blue livery but unfortunately doesn't hold any stickers or logos due to the engine being rushed in anticipation of the first appearance back at the Embsay & Bolton Abbey diesel gala. Seen here waiting to depart Embsay with the 09.00 to Bolton Abbey on 11 October 2014.

Above: The first working for the recently restored No. 37294 is seen here on the Embsay & Bolton Abbey Steam Railway at Holywell Holt. The locomotive had been in restoration for around four years and to celebrate its return the railway organised a special diesel gala event. Seen here looking well with no numbers, logos or nameplate on 11 October 2014.

Above: English Electric No. 37109 thrashes past Burrs Country Park on the East Lancashire Railway while working the 18.05 service to Rawtenstall. The Class 37 is based at Bury on the ELR and is seen here taking part in the diesel gala. Photographed on 5 July 2014. Visiting locomotive No. 37324 was on the rear.

Above: Class 56 diesel locomotives, otherwise known as 'Grids', are very rare in preservation after the sale of former No. 56057 in May 2007. No. 56057 is seen here on the Nene Valley Railway after being purchased from EWS at Immingham in 2004. The locomotive was based at Wansford on the Nene Valley, where it was restored and repainted into its Large Logo blue. Seen here on 18 September 2005. The Class 56 is now owned by Devon & Cornwall Railways (DCR) and has been renumbered to 56311.

Opposite below: Class 47 No. 47401 named *North Eastern* sits in the sun at Swanwick Junction on the Midland Railway Centre awaiting its next duty. The locomotive, which was preserved in 1993 after being purchased by the No. 47401 project, was transferred from Immingham to the Midland Railway Centre after having some repairs. It hauled its first preserved train on 17 July 1993.

Above: The only Class 58 in preservation is No. 58016, seen here sitting in Barrow Hill Roundhouse getting major repairs. The 58 is seen supporting Fertis livery after being exported to France on 14 May 2005, however the loco returned to the UK a year later when it arrived home on 25 May 2006. To add to this, the loco was purchased by the C58LG on 28 June 2010. Seen here on Saturday 18 April 2015.

Below: The Keighley & Worth Valley shed at Haworth sees two visiting locomotives having a rest from taking part in the diesel gala. Nos 31466 and 33103 await their next run down the valley and is spotted here on 27 May 2012.

Above: No. 50015 *Valiant* sits at Bury Bolton Street on the East Lancashire Railway after arriving with a service from Rawtenstall. Seen here on Saturday 4 July 2015. The class are known as 'Hoovers'.

Below: Brush Type 4 No. 47580 powers past Burrs Country Park on the East Lancashire Railway. The locomotive was a special guest to the railway's summer diesel gala and was spotted here on 5 July 2014.

Above: Privately owned chopper No. 20142 is seen powering past Darnholm on the North Yorkshire Moors Railway with the first service of the day to Pickering. Seen here taking part in the unsuccessful diesel gala on 27 June 2015.

Opposite below: Based at the Bo'ness & Kinniel Railway is SRPS-owned 26024 as it arrives into Irwell Vale on the East Lancashire Railway. The locomotive was a special guest for the diesel gala event and is seen here on 9 September 2006.

Above: One of only thirteen allocated to the Scottish Region, due to being fitted with single-line token catcher recesses in the cab sides, was No. 25901 – also known as No. 25262 (D7612). The locomotive was withdrawn from BR on 16 March 1987 and was purchased by Harry Needle Railroad Company (HNRC) in September 1989. Seen here after being sold to the South Devon Diesel Traction Group in 1999 as it departs away from Buckfastleigh with a service to Totnes. Photographed here on 10 June 2006.

Above: No. 26038 is seen sitting at Heywood on the East Lancashire Railway as a special guest to the 2015 summer diesel gala. Photographed here in the sun awaiting time to depart with the 2J67 14.51 Heywood to Rawtenstall service. Seen here on Sunday 5 July 2015.

Above: Crompton No. 33035 climbs away from Orton Mere on the Nene Valley Railway with a service to Peterborough. The locomotive was a special guest to the railways diesel gala and is seen here on 27 September 2014.

Opposite below: No. 31108 arrives into Oxenhope on the Keighley & Worth Valley Railway to attend the diesel gala, seen here on 6 June 2008. The loco, which was withdrawn from BR service in September 1991, was stored at Scunthorpe until purchased by the A1A Locomotives Limited group and moved to the Midland Railway Centre at Butterly. The locomotive hauled its first passenger service in preservation for the first time on 24 June 2000.

Above: Mirlees Pioneer No. 37901 (D6580) powers away from Glyndyfrdwy on the Llangollen Railway after a brief pause. The service was bound for Llangollen and captured here on 17 March 2007. The Class 37 was originally numbered 37150 but was chosen for the initial 37/9 series, which was going to be a test bed for the proposed Class 38. The Class 38 never happened.

Opposite below: Purchased in 2000 by the Scottish Thirty Seven Group was No. 37025 Inverness TMD, which is seen here some fifteen years on looking amazing as it sits at Bury Bolton Street on the East Lancashire Railway's summer diesel gala. The locomotive had just arrived from the depot ready to work the service to Heywood, where, unfortunately, the locomotive suffered some serious problems. Seen here on Saturday 4 July 2015.

Above: Nos 56057 and 56098 scream towards Yarwell on the Nene Valley Railway with a service to Peterborough. The train was captured here on 3 March 2007. Both locos have now been sold for commercial use and are main line registered again. No. 56098 is based at UKRL at Leicester and No. 56057 (now 56311) is based at Washwood Heath.

Above: Sounding amazing as Teddy Bear D9539 powers away from the swing bridge at Preston Docks on the Ribble Steam Railway with No. 66849 on the rear dead in tow. The locomotive, which is based at the railway, was participating in the diesel gala. The locomotive arrived at the railway from the Gloucester & Warwickshire railway in 2005.

Below: English Electric No. 37250 is seen sitting at Redmire on the Wensleydale Railway. The locomotive arrived at its new home after being removed from the nearby Eden Valley Railway at Warcop. The locomotive burst back into life on Friday 30 March 2012 after almost ten years out of service. Seen here on 18 June 2014.

Above: No. 46010 arrives into Glyndyfrdwy with a service to Carrog on the Llangollen Railway. The locomotive was withdrawn in 1984 at Gateshead depot in Newcastle after various power unit defects were found. The locomotive was purchased by the Llangollen Railway Diesel Group in 1993, where it arrived on 6 May 1994. The locomotive is now based at the Great Central Railway North in Ruddington after being removed from the railway on 5 December 2009.

Below: The Deltic Preservation Society Limited No. 55009 (D9009) *Alycidon* powers away from Irwell Vale on the East Lancashire Railway. The locomotive was visiting the railway for the summer diesel gala and was spotted here making some noise on 5 July 2014.

Above: No. 31271 thrashes past Burrs Country Park while working the shuttle service to Ramsbottom from Bury on the East Lancashire Railway. The locomotive, which was purchased from EWS at Toton depot, was moved on Thursday 28 May 1998 to the Midland Railway Centre. The locomotive burst into life for the first time in preservation on Sunday 31 March 2002 at 21.30. Seen here looking immaculate on 5 July 2014.

Above: Following on from the previous image, D5600 left the East Lancashire Railway to attend the Northern Rail Newton Heath depot open day, where it received a new nameplate – *Newton Heath TMD*. The locomotive was moved to the Embsay & Bolton Abbey Steam Railway after the event and has being successful at the small Yorkshire dales railway. Seen here at Embsay station awaiting departure with the 10.00 to Bolton Abbey on 11 October 2014.

Opposite below: Built at Brush Traction in Loughborough and released for service on 24 March 1960 was D5600, otherwise known as Nos 31179 or 31435. The loco was condemned from main line service and therefore withdrawn from service on 1 November 1995. However, the locomotive was sold on 31 December 1999 to a private individual and moved to the East Lancashire Railway for repairs and repaint. The locomotive is seen here on the East Lancashire Railway at Burrs Country Park with a service bound for Bury. Seen here on 17 February 2007.

Above: Owned by the Pioneer Diesel Group and based at Barrow Hill Roundhouse is No. 45060 *Sherwood Forester*, seen here thrashing towards Goathland on the North Yorkshire Moors Railway diesel gala on 27 June 2015.

Below: Based at the Spa Valley Railway at Tunbridge Wells is Crompton Class 33 No. 33065, seen here with No. 31271 on the Nene Valley Railway heading for Wansford on 3 March 2007. The Class 33 is owned by the South East Locomotive Group and is currently named *Sealion*.

Following on from the previous image, here we can again see No. 33065, this time working alone while heading down the Nene Valley bound for Wansford with a service from Peterborough. The loco was a star guest to the diesel gala and is seen coasting down the line on 3 March 2007.

Above: D6809, otherwise known as No. 37109, sits at Irwell Vale railway station on the East Lancashire Railway awaiting the green flag of the guard. The locomotive arrived at the railway in 2008 and before you know it the locomotive was seen running around supporting the ex-EWS livery. The locomotive was captured here on 16 March 2008. The loco has now since been painted into BR Blue.

Below: Following on from the previous image is No. 37109, seen here arriving into Ramsbottom with a service to Heywood. The locomotive had just been released from the paint shop after receiving a new coat of paint and is one of the railway's popular performers. Seen here on 30 May 2009.

Above: Based at Barrow Hill Roundhouse in Derbyshire is No. 33108, seen here at Oxenhope shed on the Keighley & Worth Valley Railway. The locomotive was visiting the railway for the diesel gala event and was photographed on 7 June 2009. The locomotive is owned by the 33/1 Preservation Company.

Below: Seen here at Llangollen is Mirlees Pioneer Class 37/9 No. 37901 as it runs around its train. The Class 37 spent its earlier years here at the Llangollen before being transferred to the East Lancashire Railway at Bury in 2008. Seen here on 17 March 2007.

Above: English Electric No. 37240 runs around its train at Llangollen on 17 March 2007. The locomotive is based at the Llangollen Railway and now holds the number 6940 and has been repainted into its new BR Blue livery.

Above: Based at the Llangollen Railway, since 1996 is No. 47449 (D1566). The locomotive is seen here departing Glyndyfrdwy, bound for Llangollen. The Type 4 has had major work and a repaint since it was seen here on 17 March 2007.

Opposite below: Built in 1961 at Swindon is Maybach warship D832 *Onslaught*. There is only two of the class preserved out of thirty-eight built. The locomotives had a very short life in traffic, seeing less than twelve years in traffic after being withdrawn in December 1972. The locomotive is a part of the Bury Hydraulic Group, but is on an extended visit to the West Somerset Railway as of 2015. Seen here at Bury next to Deltic No. 55022, or D9000, on 3 June 2007.

Above: On long-term hire to the East Lancashire Railway is EWS-liveried No. 31466, seen here working a service to Rawtenstall from Heywood. The locomotive is based at the Dean Forest Railway and is owned by the Dean Forest Diesel Association. Seen here taking part in the diesel gala on 8 March 2015.

Above: Privately owned Class 37/1 No. 37146 is seen looking a mess in its fading Civil Engineers yellow-and-grey at Kirkby Stephen East Railway. The locomotive has since been removed from the railway and has been transferred across the hills to the nearby Wensleydale Railway at Leeming Bar. The locomotive is now being restored and repaired. Seen here on 4 June 2007.

Opposite below: Normally seen at the National Railway Museum is Deltic No. 55002. However, it was seen here passing Otterburn near Hellifield while working the 5Z64 York National Railway Museum to Carnforth steam town empty coaching stock move for West Coast Railways Company. The locomotive is main line registered and works several railtours and stock moves. Seen here on 1 February 2014.

Above: English Electric Class 37/5 No. 37518 is pictured at Wansford on the Nene Valley Railway near Peterborough awaiting its next duty. The locomotive is seen supporting its Railfreight Red Stripe livery and is privately owned. The locomotive has since been sold and has been mainline registered for use on West Coast Railway services around Scotland. Seen here on 29 March 2009.

Opposite below: Having a very short life after being built in 1962 was Hymek D7076 after being withdrawn from service in May 1973. One of the East Lancashire Railway's popular locomotives, as evidenced by the window-hanging enthusiasts ready for the Maybach engine to be roared wide open as it passes Burrs. Seen here on 5 July 2014.

Above: Teddy Bear D9531 powers its mixed-goods freight towards Bury as it passes Burrs on the East Lancashire Railway. The Class 14 arrived at the East Lancashire Railway during 1987 supporting NCB dark blue livery and was used as a shunting locomotive before getting a major overhaul in 1997. Seen here on 8 March 2015.

Above: Main line-certified No. 40145 (345) powers its mixed-goods train passes Little Burrs on the East Lancashire Railway. The locomotive was the first of the final fifty-four Class 40s constructed with the centre headcode panel. Due to damage after a derailment in Stourton Yard at Leeds, the class was withdrawn from service on 10 June 1983. The loco was then secured for preservation and arrived onto the East Lancs on 16 February 1984.

Opposite below: English Electric No. 50008 *Thunderer* worked its last train in November 1991 before being withdrawn in June 1992, becoming the forty-sixth member of its class to be withdrawn having successfully worked over twenty-four years of active service. The locomotive is seen here sitting next to a pair of Class 56 diesel locomotives in the yard at Wansford on the Nene Valley Railway. The locomotive was a star guest to the railway's diesel gala, but due to a failure it never moved. Seen here on 24 April 2013.

Above: BR Sulzer Type 4 diesel locomotives were built at Derby Works between 1959 and 1960. They were nicknamed 'Peaks' because they were named after British mountains – there are only two of the class preserved and here we can see No. 44008 (D8) depart from Darley Dale on the Peak Rail Railway at Matlock. The other of the class, No. 44004 (D4), is based at the Midland Railway Centre. Seen here heading for Matlock on Saturday 18 April 2015.

Above: D7076 powers past Burrs Country Park with a service bound for Rawtenstall. Seen here on the East Lancashire Railways diesel gala running on its home railway on Saturday 4 July 2015.

Below: No. 40135 is one of the twenty Class 40s to be built with the split box route indicator. The locomotive entered traffic on 10 March 1961 and was withdrawn as surplus to requirement on 16 December 1986. The Class 40 arrived at its new home at Bury in 1988, where it has been a very popular performer for the railway. It is seen here working shuttles between Ramsbottom and Bury as it passes Burrs on 15 October 2010.

Above: Looking in a very sorry state is No. 31418 as it sits in the bottom yard at the Midland Railway Centre at Swanwick Junction. The Class 31 is undergoing a severe overhaul and repaint. The loco, which was built in 1959 at Brush Traction in Loughborough, is owned by the A1A Locomotives Limited group. Seen here on 20 May 2007.

Below: Based at Barrow Hill Roundhouse near Chesterfield is Deltic No. 55019, is seen here screaming past Burrs Country Park and caravan site while working on the East Lancashire Railway. The locomotive entered service in 1961 for British Rail and was based at Haymarket depot in Edinburgh. It was the last Deltic to receive a name, receiving it in a ceremony at Glasgow Central Railway Station in September 1965 and being named *Royal Highland Fusillier*. The locomotive was withdrawn on 31 December 1981 and purchased by the Deltic Preservation Society (DPS) the same year.

Above: The East Lancashire Railway-based Class 24 D5054 is seen on the rear of a service bound for Heywood. The locomotive is currently undergoing a major body and engine overhaul. Seen here on 9 May 2005.

Opposite below: BR Large Logo No. 37314 arrives into Buckfastleigh with a service from Totnes. The Class 37 is currently at Washwood Heath undergoing a major overhaul and being repainted into BR Blue. Seen here on the South Devon Railway on 10 June 2006.

Above: BR Green-liveried No. 20166 is seen at Leeming Bar on the Wensleydale Railway. The locomotive is receiving major attention and is owned by Harry Needle (HNRC). Captured here on 18 July 2014.

Above: Mirlees Pioneer Class 37/9 No. 37906 is seen sitting at Kidderminster station on the Severn Valley Railway with Hoover No. 50026. The Class 37 is now based at UKRL Leicester, where it is used as a yard shunter. Seen here on 10 October 2009.

Above: After being built at Crewe Works in 1966, BR Type 4 CO-CO No. 47643, otherwise known as No. 47269 or D1970, powers past Burrs while working the 2J67 14.51 Heywood to Rawtenstall service. The locomotive, visiting the East Lancashire Railway for the summer 2015 diesel gala, is based at the Bo'ness & Kinniel Railway and owned by the Scottish Railway Preservation Society (SRPS). Seen here on Saturday 4 July 2015.

Opposite below: The Class 40 Preservation Society partnered up with Compass Railtours to work a railtour from Holyhead to Durham. Class 40 No. 40145 was the leading locomotive and is seen here passing Horesfall Tunnel near Todmorden with the 1Z40 07.36 Holyhead to Durham outward leg. Seen here on Monday 25 May 2009.

Above: BR Large Logo-liveried No. 50015 *Valiant* sits at Ramsbottom station, awaiting time to depart, with the 2J56 09.43 to Bury shuttle service. The locomotive is one of the eighteen preserved of its class and was withdrawn from main line service on 5 June 1992. Not long after the withdrawal the locomotive was sent to Bury on the East Lancashire Railway in October 1992. Seen here on Sunday 5 July 2015.

Below: After the failure of No. 40135 (D335) at Summerseat, No. 55009 (D9009) was sent from Ramsbottom to rescue the locomotive and work the train back to Ramsbottom. The train arrived at Ramsbottom some 30 minutes late and was therefore dragged back to Bury by double-headed peds No. 31466 leading No. 31271. Here we can see the train approaching Burrs on the late-running Heywood service. Captured here on 5 July 2014.

Above: No. 56003 powers towards Wansford on the Nene Valley railway with classmate No. 56098 in tow. The Class 56 was saved from scrap when it was purchased for preservation from CF Booths at Rotherham in 2004. The locomotive was moved to the MOD site at Ashchurch near Gloucester, where a full overhaul was undertaken. The locomotive made its debut at the nearby Gloucester & Warwickshire Railway, from there it started travelling around the country to many other preserved railways before it was sold on for commercial usage. It is now main line registered and runs as No. 56312.

Below: Sitting in the sun at Eastleigh Works open day is newly liveried Class 50/1 No. 50135 in its new Loadhaul livery. The Class 50 is actually numbered No. 50035 and is named *Ark Royal*. The English Electric design was built in 1968 and is currently based at Kidderminster on the Severn Valley Railway. Seen here on 23 May 2009.

Above: Double-headed Mirlees Pioneers Class 37/9 Nos 37906 and 37901 pass Townsend Fold level crossings after just departing from Rawtenstall with a service bound for Heywood. The train was captured here on 29 June 2008.

Opposite below: No. 47376, otherwise known as D1895, is owned by The Brush Type 4 Fund and is permanently based at the Gloucester & Warwickshire Railway. The locomotive is seen here passing Hailes while working a service to Toddington from Cheltenham Racecourse. Seen here on 2 April 2005.

Above: Deltic No. 55022 arrives into Irwell Vale on the East Lancashire Railway with the 13.13 Rawtenstall to Heywood service. Captured here on 16 March 2008.

Above: With a maximum speed of 90 mph, English Electric Bo-Bo No. 73129 (E6036) powers a freight train towards Cheltenham Racecourse as it passes under Hailes Bridge. The locomotive is one of a class of forty-nine electro-diesels and introduced in 1962 to work on the southern region. To add to this, the locos were built at the Vulcan Foundry and can either use their own internal diesel engine or pick up a 750-volt third rail supply. Seen here on 2 April 2005.

Above: No. 47105 (D1693) is owned by the Brush Type 4 Fund and is based at the Gloucester Warwickshire Railway. The locomotive, which was purchased from Crewe in January 1994, arrived at the railway in April the same year. Seen here working a mixed-freight train as it passes Hailes, bound for Cheltenham Racecourse, on 2 April 2005.

Opposite below: Class 24 locomotives were built by British Rail at Crewe in 1960. Here we can see privately owned No. 24081 (D5081) power its mixed-goods train towards Toddington on the Gloucester & Warwickshire Railway. Seen here on 2 April 2005.

Above: Mainline Blue-liveried No. 37219 powers past Hailes with a mixed-goods train to Cheltenham Spa. The locomotive has now been sold out of preservation to Colas Rail for mainline use. Seen here working on the Gloucester Warwickshire Railway diesel gala on 2 April 2005.

Opposite below: Entering into traffic at the end of 1967 were the Class 50 locomotives. Here we can see No. 50019 *Ramillies* at Dereham running around its train after just arriving from Wymondham. The locomotive was withdrawn from service in late 1990 due to generator flashover damage and then purchased by the Class 50 Locomotive Association in September 1991 and moved to the Spa Valley Railway at Tunbridge Wells on 7 January 1992. However, the loco was moved again to the Mid-Norfolk Railway at Dereham, where it arrived on 21 May 1999.

Above: After having engine repairs at Carnforth, national treasure ex-Res/EWS royal train loco No. 47798 *Prince William* worked several charters for West Coast Railways. It's seen here returning its empty coaching stock back to Carnforth as it passes Eldroth on the Little North Western line from a previous day's railtour. The locomotive is based at the National Railway Musuem in York. Seen here on 12 April 2009.

Above: The Deltic Preservations Society's Deltic D9009 *Alycidon* is seen passing Hellifield while hauling the 1Z55 Crewe to Carlisle 'The Winter Settler' Pathfinder railtour. The train is seen here on 28 December 2014.

Above: Being built between 1961 and 1962 by English Electric were the Class 55 Deltics. Here we see No. 55016 (D9016) *Gordon Highlander*, which was purchased by the Deltic 9000 Fund and loaned to Porterbrook Leasing. As of November 2007, the locomotive was based at Peak Rail near Matlock in Derbyshire. The locomotive was then sold by a private member to Harry Needle Rail Company for spot hire as a business venture. The locomotive is now based at the Great Central Railway in Loughborough. Seen here at Rowsley on the Peak Rail line on 20 May 2007.

Opposite below: Known as the BRCW Type 2 locomotives are the Class 26. Here we can see No. 26007 power away from Loughborough while working a train to Leicester North on the Great Central Railway. The Class 26 is privately owned and seen here on 17 April 2010.

Above: Repainted No. 55016 (D9016) is seen here at Bury while arriving on the tail end with a service from Heywood. Deltic No. 55019 was on the front of the train. Seen here on 15 October 2011.

Above: No. 40106 (D306) was the second Class 40 to enter preservation but the first to be returned to operational condition. The locomotive is owned by Neil Bowden and is based at Washwood Heath in Birmingham. The locomotive is seen here nearly at journeys end as it arrives into Wansford with a service from Peterborough on the Nene Valley Railway. Seen here on 3 March 2007.

Opposite below: Here we see Peak D123 climb out of Loughborough on the Great Central Railway while working a service to Leicester North. D123 was built at Crewe Works in 1961 and released to traffic at Derby on 28 October of that year. The locomotive was purchased for preservation in 1991 by the Humberside Locomotive Preservation Group (now named No. 5305 *Locomotive Association*) and moved to their base on the outskirts of Hull at Dairycoates on 23 May 1992. The locomotive arrived at the Great Central Railway in 1998 and is permanently based at the railway. Photographed here on 17 April 2010.

Above: Triple-headed Teddy Bears D9516, D9518 and D9520 power through Castor while working the 11.32 Wansford to Peterborough service. The locomotives were taking part in the Nene Valley Railway's diesel gala event and are pictured here on 3 March 2007.

Below: East Lancashire Railway resident No. 33109 *Captain Bill Smith RNR* blasts past Burrs Country Park while double-heading along with Scottish Preservation Society's Class 26 No. 26038 *Tom Clift* as they work the 14.51 2J67 Heywood to Rawtenstall service. Seen here on Friday 3 July 2015.

Above: Withdrawn in 2003, after arriving back from its year's holiday in France, was No. 37037 (D6737 *Loch Treig*). The locomotive was purchased by Harry Needle Railroad Company (HNRC) but later sold to the Devon Diesel Society at the beginning of 2004. The locomotive arrived at the South Devon Railway Buckfastleigh site after being restored at Barrow Hill in July 2004. The locomotive is seen here departing Keighley while visiting the Keighley & Worth Valley Railway for their 2008 diesel gala. The service was the 10.34 to Oxenhope and is seen here waking the residents with an eventful departure. Seen here on 6 June 2008.

Below: EWS-liveried No. 37418 arrives into Ramsbottom in the snow as it works a Heywood-bound service from Rawtenstall. The Class 37 is based at the East Lancashire Railway and is captured here on 9 January 2010 as it takes part in the winter diesel gala.

Above: Owned by the Stratford 47 Group is No. 47596, seen here sporting its Network South East livery as it tails a Rawtenstall service past Heap Bridge. The locomotive was visiting the East Lancashire Railway for the diesel gala among many other guests. The Class 47 is based at the Mid-Norfolk Railway in Dereham and is seen here on 6 July 2013.

Above: The 125 Group took custody of the HST Prototype vehicle No. 41001 when they struck a deal with the National Railway Museum at York back in 2012. The locomotive was moved to East Midlands Trains' Neville Hill depot on the outskirts of Leeds, where work was carried out for its restoration. On 1 July 2013 the locomotive fired up its S508 engine, meaning it was the first time in thirty years the locomotive had a running engine. The locomotive moved to the Great Central Railway North at Ruddington on 18 September 2013 and on 31 May 2014 made its first test run since its retirement from service. The loco broke history when on 15 November 2014 it hauled its first passenger working train in thirty-eight years when it joined East Midlands Trains railtour 'The Screaming Valenta' down the Great Central Railway. The train is seen here arriving into Ruddington on its first running day in preservation for the public on Sunday 24 May 2015.

Opposite below: No. 40012 (D212) was withdrawn from traffic by BR on 4 April 1986 and was bought by the Class 40 appeal in June 1988. The locomotive is based at the Midland Railway Centre in Butterly and is seen sitting at Barrow Hill next to sister No. 40013(D213) on Saturday 18 April 2015.

Above: No. 73110 (E6016) is seen sitting in the yard at Ruddington among Nos 25279 (D7629) and 31162 (5580) awaiting their next turn of call. The Class 73 is owned by the English Electric Preservation Group and is seen here on Sunday 24 May 2015.

Above: East Lancashire Railway resident Hymek D7076 powers towards Burrs as it works a service bound for Heywood. Seen here on 5 July 2014.

Opposite below: Normally seen at the National Railway Musuem is No. 55002 *The King's Own Yorkshire Light Infantry*, however it is pictured here passing Shrivenham on the Great Western mainline while in charge of the 10.54 0Z53 Kidderminster SVR to Didcot GWS light engine movement on Thursday 15 May 2014.

Above: The Nene Valley Railway at Wansford saw No. 31108 power the 10.00 Wansford to Peterborough service. The Class 31 was taking part in the railways diesel gala event with other visiting locomotives including Nos 33035, 56081 and more. Seen here making some noise on 27 September 2014.

Below: Numbered N.C.B 38 is Teddy Bear D9513, seen here arriving into Embsay station. The locomotive arrived at the railway in 1987 after being sold from Ashington Colliery in Northumberland and is seen taking part in the diesel gala on 11 October 2014.

Above: No. 20907, otherwise known as No. 20205, sits in the yard at Swanwick Junction on the Midland Railway Centre with sister class No. 20189. The locomotive is owned by the Class 20 Locomotive Society. Seen here on 20 May 2007.

Below: The Llangollen Railway in Denbighshire is 10 miles in length and runs from Llangollen to Corwen through the scenic Dee Valley. Here we see resident No. 47449 (D1566) running around its train at Llangollen after just arriving with a service from Carrog on 17 March 2007.

Above: Based at Peak Rail is No. 31270, seen here at Rowsley running around its train after just arriving from Matlock. The locomotive is now a permanent resident to the railway after moving for the Colne Valley Railway. The locomotive has since had a repaint and now supports the blue and grey Regional Railways colours. Seen here on 20 May 2007.

Above: English Electric Hoovers No. 50029 *Renown* and No. 50030 *Repulse* are seen sitting in the yard at Rowsley on the Peak Rail line. No. 50029 worked its last train in January 1992 due to power unit damage and became the forty-third of its class to be withdrawn after over twenty-three years active service. The locomotive, along with No. 50030, has been purchased by the Renown Repulse Restoration Group and was moved to Rowsley. On the other hand, No. 50030 worked its last train in February 1992 and was withdrawn from service in April the same year due to main generator damage. The loco became the forty-fifth of its class to be withdrawn.

Opposite below: Seen sporting SWT Blue livery, with no numbers or decals, is No. 33046 (D6564) *Merlin*. The Class 33 is now based at the East Lancashire Railway at Bury, but is seen here at the Midland Railway Centre in Butterly on 20 May 2007.

Above: D8132 sits next to sister No. 20001 at Swanwick Junction on the Midland Railway Centre. The locomotive is now mainline registered and runs as No. 20132, on hire to GBRF for moving the London Underground Tube stock. BR Blue-liveried No. 20001 is based at the Midland Railway Centre and is owned by the Class 20 Locomotive Society.

Opposite below: Railfreight-liveried No. 31108 powers away from Swanwick Junction on the Midland Railway Centre with a service to Riddings. The Class 31 was working among a gathering of Class 20 diesel locomotives that were taking part in Chopperfest. Seen here on 20 May 2007.

Above: Here we can see a trio of ex-BR diesel locomotives. D1015 *Western Champion* sits next to No. 45060 *Sherwood Forester* and, on the end, No. 55022 *Royal Scots Grey*, all sitting in Eastleigh Works for the open day event. Seen here on 25 May 2009.

Above: No. 45041 *Royal Tank Regiment* was built at Crewe Works in 1962, released on 25 June the same year and was based at Derby. The locomotive suffered traction motor problems while working a Peak Forest stone train and was therefore taken out of service on 18 May 1988. The locomotive was later condemned out of service at Thornaby depot in Middlesbrough on 8 June 1988. The locomotive is now owned by the Peak Locomotive Company and arrived onto the railway at Midland Railway Centre in 1996. It can now be found at the Great Central Railway in Loughborough. Seen here on 20 May 2007.

Opposite below: Double-headed 20s Nos 20154 and 20132 power towards Riddings just after departing Swanwick Junction. Seen here on 20 May 2007.

Above: No. 20154 (D8154) paired with No. 20007 (D8007) sit in front of No. 20189 and No. 20907 (20205) at the Midland Railway Centre's site at Swanwick Junction, all awaiting their next turn to trip down the line to Riddings. The Class 20 diesel locomotives were built between 1957 and 1968. Seen here on 20 May 2007.

Above: Mainline-registered No. 20189 sits next to now mainline-registered and renumbered No. 20205, still No. 20907 here, as they sit in the yard at Swanwick Junction. Seen here on 20 May 2007.

Above: Based at the Birmingham Railway Musuem at Tyseley is Vintage Trains-owned No. 47773. The locomotive, which is mainline registered, is used for railtours and train heat. Seen here working the 06.26 1Z90 Tyseley to Carlisle Vintage Trains 'The Cumbrian Jubilee' railtour. The Class 47 only worked the train as far as Hellifield Goods Loop, where LMS Jubilee Class 5690 *Leander* took over the tour. Seen here on Saturday 21 March 2015.

Opposite below: After just arriving into Llangollen with a service from Carrog is No. 37240 (6940). The locomotive is based here at Llangollen and has recently had a major overhaul and repaint into BR Blue. Seen sitting here on 17 March 2007.

Vintage Train ran a special working using both No. 47773 and No. 4464 *Bittern* on 'The Cumbrian Ranger', which ran from Tyseley Warwick Road via Wolverhampton and the West Coast mainline, and back via the Settle & Carlisle Railway. The return leg of the tour is seen here as No. 47773 helps No. 4464 *Bittern* out with the small climb to Newsholme on the Ribble Valley line while working the 1Z46 Carlisle to Tyseley. Seen here on 15 March 2014.